THE MANAGEMENT PLAYBOOK

Be the common denominator of success

CONTENTS

For additional information, please contact The Business Blueprint at:

155 No. 400 W. Ste 180
SLC, UT 84103

801.214.9689

info@thebizblueprint.com www.
TheBizBlueprint.com

Vision is one of the most overlooked aspects of a business. Is your business communicating intentionally?

Most business owners know they need to work on their business. Some of these same business owners don't know what working on the busines is or how to create the time and space to do it.

Productive relationships are at the core of any successful business. Are you putting in the time to build productive relationships in your business?

The outcomes of a business either happen by accident or by choice. What type of business do you want?

the day I realized *I* was the common denominator of my team's *failure*

Imagine that you have a team that would come in on a Saturday if you asked them to, love what they do, and are willing to fight for your business. Some of you may already have this at some level. Others may snort and say, "Yeah right."

You see, I used to think like the later. I had an under-performing team. They were lazy, unmotivated, stupid, C-teamers. And they all had one thing in common. They all had a shitty boss. Unfortunately, that shitty boss was me.

It was a real come-to-Jesus moment when I realized that my team was underperforming and I was about to get fired. After talking with some time and talking with my team, I realized that I needed to make some changes. To make a long story short, I got some help to make me a better leader and a manager.

The result?

My team went from mediocre to one of the best teams in my region—and I got promoted.

What changed? Me.

I mentioned that I educated myself and it was a huge help to me. You can probably relate to the fact that we often get thrown into leadership positions with little or no training on how to effectively lead our teams. In the end, you are left to figure it out for yourself.

Figuring it out for yourself often leads to a leadership paradigm that makes you cynical, mistrustful, and angry at your team. As a business owner, you have enough to worry about in your business without carrying around that baggage.

I am putting this playbook together for all the leaders who have been thrown to the fire. I want to help business owners with the knowledge that they need to create an engaged team—just like someone did for me many years ago.

High-performing teams need a high-performing leader to take them to the next level. Are you ready to be that leader?

Enjoy the playbook and keep it handy because you will probably need to reference it again and again as you learn and implement the tactics in this book.

To your success,

BRANDON ALLEN – Here's the skinny on me. I am a business coach and consultant with the Business Blueprint and Business FastTrack. I have never saved a baby from a burning building or scaled Mt. Everest. However, through years of running different operations, I have an uncanny knack for seeing other business owners' vision and putting that into an actionable plan for success. I love business and everything that comes with it.

When I am not coaching or writing, I, along with my wife and 4 cute little girls, live in Salt Lake City, Utah. When asked to describe myself, I will tell you that I am "funny, charming, interesting, and handsome," all of which claims are highly questionable other than the first. I enjoy triathlons, sports, music, hanging out with family, and reading when I am not busy helping others capitalize on their potential.

BRANDON ALLEN

The correct approach for your vision is to use it as an ongoing tool for teaching, training, con-fronting, inspiring, and moving your team.

You can have all the management tools in the world, but they won't make a bit of difference in your business if you don't have the right habits in your business.

There are three specific management habits that are vital to running a thriving operation: communicating your vision, working on your business, and building relationships.

communicating your vision

The first habit is a simple one to understand but not always easy to incorporate into your business. It deals with the habit of communicating the vision. It's important for you as a business owner to paint the big picture for your team at every possible opportunity.

How often are you communicating the vision with your team?

How would your business improve if you and your team were crystal clear on the direction of your business? What are some possible outcomes that you can think of?

If you forget about your vision, your team will, too.

When I work with a client on their vision, I ask a few questions about how well they communicate the vision and how they use it in their business. Typically I get similar responses from people like, "Yeah we have those things," "We've discussed them with our team already," and so on.

Business owners tend to treat communicating their vision as a one-time event. As soon as it's checked off the list, no one ever hears about it again. The correct approach for your vision is to use it as an ongoing tool for teaching, training, confronting, inspiring, and moving your team.

Lorin Woolfe the authority on leadership said it perfectly:

"Stay . . . focused on your message, repeating the same mantra until you can't stand the sound of your own voice and then repeating it some more, because just when you start to become bored witless with the message, it's probably starting to seep into the organization."

You can't just state your vision once and expect it to create the type of power you want overnight. You must constantly reinforce the message. Your employees aren't performing up to standards? Let them know how this affects the vision of your business. Are you training people? Make your vision part of the training all of the time.

When you get into the habit of directing your team through your vision-inspired objectives, you start to create a big picture that everyone on your team can see and eventually buy into.

EXERCISE IN DISCOVERY

Below are some questions to ponder during your work on the business time or you can take some time and do this now.

1. Are you clear on your business vision?

_____

_____

_____

_____

2. What can you do as a leader to be a better communicator of the big picture vision?

_____

_____

_____

_____

3. How would understanding the big picture help your team to perform better?

_____

_____

_____

_____

working on your business

The second habit of your business is one of those things that's easy to understand but hard to live. It's deals with working on your business. When I say working on your business, I mean systematically, methodically, and in manner that produces results for your business.

What does working on the business look like? Working on your business is about looking at your business from a 30,000-foot viewpoint and assessing where you are at.

This process includes looking at your systems, your results, and your people and asking yourself how you can improve in each of these areas. I talked earlier about managing by objectives. Reviewing objectives' progress is a great activity to do during this time since it forces you to look at the systems and people that help you get the results that you are looking for.

Here are a few guidelines for working on the business:

1. Set up a consistent time that you work on your business every week.

2. Set a specific agenda with that time of what you want to accomplish.

3. Do this activity in a place where you can be productive. This is not always your office. I like to work on certain things at a coffee shop or outside where I can be free of distraction.

4. Be present. This is the time to turn off your phone, e-mail, and so on. You need to be 100 percent focused on what you are doing.

Who Has Time For This Stuff?

You may think that the above guidelines sound great and that you would love to do them, but you may also be asking yourself how you can fit this into an already-busy schedule of working in the business. My suggestion to you is very fancy and very complex . . . wait for it . . . here it comes . . . *make time*. That's it. If you don't have time to work on your business, then you need to make time.

Making time for working on your business may not be easy at first. In reality, nothing ever worth doing comes easy to us right off the bat. It takes a little dedication and a little work.

Take running for example. I was once a distance runner in college. By the end of my college career, I was putting in around 100 miles per week and could run a marathon like it was no big deal.

The journey to get there started the summer before my sophomore year of high school with me "running" 10 minutes. "If I could just run three miles" is what I told myself.

The good news is that it doesn't have to be hard forever. Pretty soon spending significant time working on your business will be like running a marathon like it was no big deal. You just know how to get it done.

While some business owners argue that working on their businesses wastes valuable time because it may take them out of an income producing activity such as doing work for a client, there is not another activity in your business that will produce more value than working on it and improving the system through which the business operates.

BENEFITS OF WORKING ON YOUR BUSINESS

Business owners that I have worked with who buy into this concept expand their business beyond what they thought possible and they work less and less in their business as a result. Are they unhappy about that? No. In fact they find that they have more money, more fulfillment, more time with their families, and more freedom.

Working on your business also enables you to create healthy environments for people to thrive in. Obviously it's important to create a great environment for your customers but what about your people? Are you overlooking the environment that they are working in?

When you create the right environment for your team, here's what you are really creating:

- A team that works proactively vs. reactively
- High-level communication where everyone is on the same page.
- An environment in which people truly enjoy what they do.
- A goal-minded team.
- A business owner who doesn't have to work as many hours in the business.
- True teamwork.

If you could have the above things working in your business consistently would you make time for it? Of course you would.

So why do we use time as an excuse?

Time isn't the real issue here. The issue is really about having a powerful enough *why* and a powerful enough *what* to guide you.

A powerful *why* comes from being plugged into the overall vision of your business and using that as a catalyst for behavior in your business. The *what* comes down to your philosophy on managing your business.

The ultimate end result for your business is management that is easy, effective, and efficient.

Time isn't the real issue here. The issue is really about having a powerful enough why *and a powerful enough* what *to guide you.*

EXERCISE IN DISCOVERY

Take some time and think through the answers to these questions about you and your business.

1. What keeps you from working on your business now?

_____

_____

_____

_____

2. How many hours a week do you ideally want to work on your business?

_____

_____

_____

_____

3. What types of big picture activities would you work on if you you set aside consistent time to get them done?

_____

_____

_____

_____

4. If you worked more on your business, how would this make you a better manager of your team and business?

_____

_____

_____

_____

building relationships

WHAT KIND OF MANAGER DO YOU WANT TO BE?

Whether you are the short-term solution (just holding the fort down until you can hire someone to replace you) or you are the long-term solution, you need to first identify what kind of manager you want to be.

Are you going to be a total hard ass that only cares about results? The compassionate people person who is always showing concern for the people that work with you? Are you going to be fun? All business? Zany? Focused? In the end, it doesn't matter as long as you are being true to yourself and you are consistent.

I can usually tell when a business owner is having an identity crisis when it comes to managing their team. They are nice and compassionate one day and direct and harsh the next. The problem with this is that is creates uncertainty in your team and they are left unsure of what they are going to get from one day to the next. This level of uncertainty erodes morale over time.

Understanding what kind of manager you want to be starts with understanding your values. What do you value as a person? What does your business value as an entity? If you don't know the answers to these questions then you can't have a consistent management philosophy.

Let's take a few minutes and address this now.

What do you value personally?

First make a list of ten things that you value.

Understanding what kind of manager you want to be starts with understanding your values.

1. _____
2. _____
3. _____
4. _____
5. _____
6. _____
7. _____
8. _____
9. _____
10. _____

Now take that list and pare that down to five. Keep in mind that this list is the five things that you value as an individual more than anything else in the world. These values are not to be compromised in any area of your life.

1. _____

2. _____

3. _____

4. _____

5. _____

Now do the same for your business.

1. _____

2. _____

3. _____

4. _____

5. _____

6. _____

7. _____

8. _____

9. _____

10. _____

Now pare this list down to five.

1. _____

2. _____

3. _____

4. _____

5. _____

If you don't know the answers to these questions then you can't have a consistent management philosophy.

As you review this list, you should be able to start identifying what your management philosophy should look like.

In a couple of sentences, describe what kind of a manager that you want to be.

_____

_____

_____

_____

Congratulations. You now have a management philosophy.

THE WONDERFUL WORLD OF CONFRONTATION

The ability to confront people does not come naturally for most people. Even people who consider themselves abrasive have a hard time taking the initiative to confront behavior.

I can remember my early days as a manager. I would rarely confront behavior in a healthy way. I wanted to be known as a nice guy. As it turns out, my complete lack of dealing with issues and being nice turned me into an asshole who doesn't care about people.

It turns out that when I expected greatness from my team, more often than not, they were great.

Have you ever literally just watched someone on your team fail right before your eyes and then you had to get rid of them for poor performance? I have, and it sucks because you know that you could have done something to intervene. They lost their job and their ability to provide for their family, but at least you were "nice" to them.

I had to change my paradigm about how I interacted with people. I decided that rather than being polite, I would be honest and confront real issues. Instead of being silent, I had conversations with my team.

The end result of my new found paradigm shift was that people liked me more not less. My people knew that I cared about their career. I wasn't going to settle for my team being mediocre. It turns out that when I expected greatness from my team, more often than not, they were great.

It all started with confronting my team in a healthy way. Here are my three tips to healthy confrontation.

1. Be timely – Good confrontation is timely. The issue needs to be addressed with your team while it is still fresh and everyone remembers the situation. Don't be the manager that is passive aggressive and waits until several small issues become one big issue. Small issues are way easier to resolve than big ones. Kill the beast while it is small.

2. Be specific – Good confrontation has no room for generalizations about an individual's character or your "feelings" about a situation. For instance, I hear things like, "I feel like you don't care" or "You always do this and that." You can't possibly know someone's feelings for sure and generalizations are never fair. What you have done in this situation is clouded the issue at hand. Instead, stick to specifics. For example, "On this date, I observed this behavior and this is what we are going to talk about in this meeting." Specifics are much harder to argue with.

3. Be professional – Being a professional is about handling confrontation with respect. This means not confronting people in public and not getting overly emotional about the confrontation—that is, yelling. Have you ever been to a place of business and watched the owner of the business dress down an employee right in front of you? We all have. It certainly lowers your opinion of the business when you see this happen.

How to Have a Productive Confrontation Meeting

You know the three guidelines of good confrontation but how do you take this a step further and create real transformation from your confrontation? For this, you need to put your coaching hat on.

That's right—your coaching hat. Most business owners forget that one of their main responsibilities as a manager is to coach their team for success.

Coaching is about inspiring your team and getting people to raise their level of performance beyond what they think is possible.

Are you doing this for your team?

Confrontation should entail creating a positive outcome with your team after the confrontation has taken place.

Here are my four steps for making this happen:

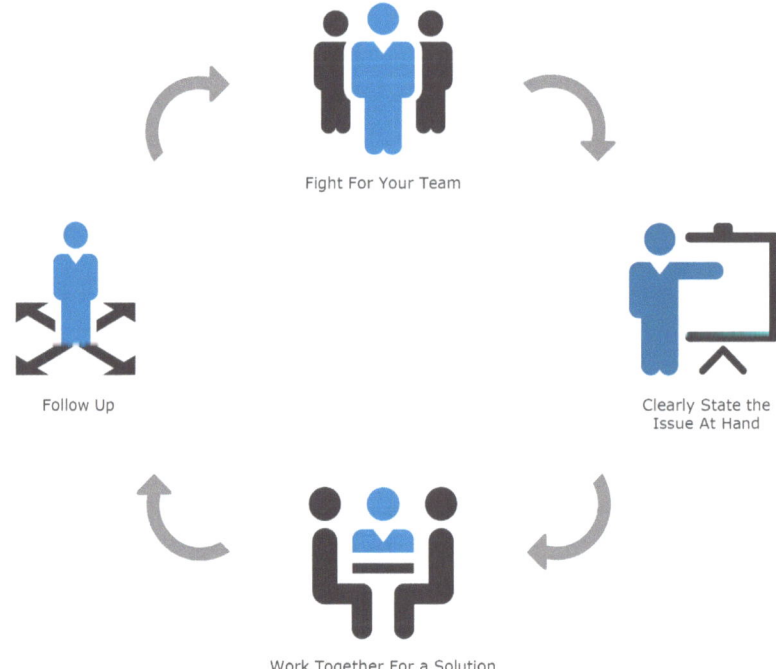

What if I told you that the way to really create an engaged team is to do the exact opposite of traditional advice?

1. **Fight for Your Team** – Let them know that you support them and have their back. Make your employee's flaws sound atypical.

2. **Clearly State the Issue at Hand** – Only state one issue. This is not the time for the laundry list of disappointment.

3. **Work Together for a Solution** – Let the person you are confronting come up with a solution to the problem at hand with your guidance.

4. **Follow Up** – Make sure the new behavior becomes a habit in its own right.

Following these steps ensures that your team knows that you are on their side and that you want them to be successful. It also creates buy in as you allow them to come up with a solution to the problem. Now they are invested in the solution. Following up lets your team know that you are serious about the issue and that they will be held accountable.

Out with the Old, in with the New

One of the first pieces of management advice that I remember getting was "Don't be friends with your employees." I was told to keep people who worked for me at an arms length. As I talk to people, like you, about this advice, it appears that I am not the only one who has been told that.

What if I told you that the way to really create an engaged team is to do the exact opposite of traditional advice?

I decided that rather than hold my team away from me and being distant (which didn't work for me), I would pull my team closer to me.

In doing so, I realized the following things:

- My team had personal goals that they were working toward that I was unaware of.
- They had lives outside of the office.
- They had hobbies, kids, etc.
- They wanted to do a great job.

Connecting with your employees seems really obvious on some levels, yet a lot of business owners and managers don't take the time to do this. I had breakfast with a friend of mine recently who told me about his boss. His boss was completely clueless that my friend had adopted a child until well after the fact.

What Happens When There Is Confrontation without Connection

If I asked you about the specific details of your team's hopes and desires and long-term goals, what could you tell me about them? You may be able to tell me a lot about your team or you may be able to tell me very little. You have to have a connection with your team if you are going to confront and coach them.

If I am your employee, what I really want to know is, do you care?

If I am your employee, what I really want to know is, do you care? As an employee, if I feel like you do care, then I will be more receptive to your input. If I feel like you don't care about me, then forget it. I will resent your confrontation and your coaching.

Think about your own life. While criticism is not always easy to take, it's much easier to accept when it you feel like it comes from someone that cares about you. You know the feedback is coming from a good place.

How do you build this trust and connect with your team? Here are a few tips that you can't implement immediately into your business.

I would argue that the most important relationship in your business is with your team.

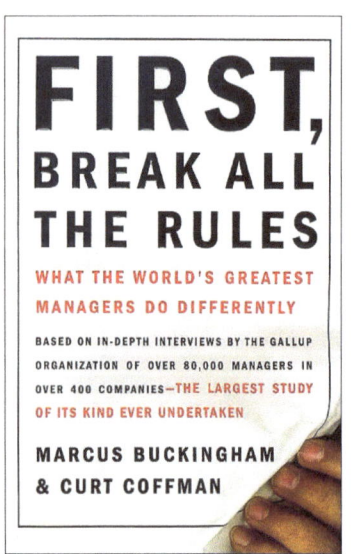

1. Always assume the best. This seems like a pretty straightforward and easy thing to do, but I am always amazed out how easily we assume the worst in our teams. Think about it this way. Have you ever had someone bring something up to you about your business that on the surface looked negative and you immediately assumed the worst about the person involved in that area of your business? We all have done this, and it's easy to do. Your team will see you care about them when they see that you are giving them the benefit of the doubt.

2. Fight for your team. Remember the coaching model? Step 1 is about being supportive. Fighting for your team is about putting your team first. Most business owners would tell you that their most important relationships in their business are with their customers. I would argue that the most important relationship in your business is with your team. If you're not sure where your team ranks in your business, ask yourself the following questions. When was the last time you asked them about their personal or career goals? When was the last time you spent meaningful one on one time? How do you review their performance?

3. Spend time with your team. If you want to connect with your team then set aside time for your team and stick to it. This time could be for training or for daily huddles or it could for going to lunch or getting a beer after work. When I first started managing, one piece of advice that I got was not to befriend your employees. I found this to be terrible and impractical advice. In fact, my team's performance is best when I spend time with them and know them on a personal level.

4. Get to know them. One tool that I have used for many years comes from the book *First, Break All the Rules*. It's a set of ten questions that provide some meaningful information into the lives of your team. These questions aren't to be taken lightly and they should be used only in the context of building a great relationship with your team and helping them take their career to the next level. This exercise is not about you, it's about them.

   a. Here are the questions:

      i. What keeps you here?

      ii. What do you think your strengths are? (skills, knowledge, talent)

      iii. What about your weaknesses?

      iv. What are your goals for your current role? (give a timeline)

      v. How often do you like to meet with me to discuss your progress? Are you the kind of person who will tell how you are feeling or do I have to ask?

vi. Do you have any personal goals or commitments you would like to tell me about?

vii. What is the best praise you have ever received? What made it so good?

viii. Have you had any productive partnerships or mentors? Why do you think these relationships worked so well for you?

ix. What are your future growth goals, your career goals? Are there any particular skills you want to learn? Are there some specific challenges you want to experience?

x. Is there anything else you want to talk about that might help us work well together?

These ten questions will give you a world of insight and allow you to make some changes on your relationship with your team for the better.

There are some rules for implementation. The first is to set the right context. This tool is about them not you. It's for their benefit, not yours. Give them a few days to fill this out but make sure you get them back in a timely manner. Once you get them back, meet one-on-one with them to discuss the answers immediately. Your team will make themselves vulnerable by answering these questions, don't leave it hanging out there for too long or you will do more harm than good.

5. Train your team. A lot of businesses rely solely on a group-training model to work with their teams. While there is a time and a place for group training, the people on your team have individual needs that shouldn't be ignored. Your individual training does not have to be every week, but it does need to be consistent. Training your team is a great way for your team to get to their next level in their work lives.

Connecting and building relationships takes time. You can't start doing all of the things listed above at once. What I would suggest is to start with the first couple of items on the above list and go from there. When you and your team is connected, your team will fight for you and your business just like you have shown that you are willing to fight for them. Your team will feel a sense of purpose and fulfillment when they are at work.

When you and your team is connected, your team will fight for you and your business just like you have shown that you are willing to fight for them.

Exercise in Discovery

Take some time and work through the following questions on building relationships as a manager.

1. How do you think your team would respond to your feedback (good and bad) if you connected with them better?

_____
_____
_____
_____

2. What keeps you from connecting with them now?

_____
_____
_____
_____

Believe it or not, the vast majority of your employees want to do a great job for you.

3. What type of culture do you want to create in your business?

_____
_____
_____
_____

4. What would your relationship be like with your team if you held them more accountable?

_____
_____
_____
_____

5. What's the first thing that you want to do to improve in this area?

_____
_____
_____
_____

OBJECTIVES, RESULTS, AND PROGRESS REPORTS

What if you came into your business and couldn't look at a profit and loss or customer stats? What if you never knew how your business was doing? Would that drive you more than a little crazy? If you're like me, then this would drive you absolutely nuts.

Your employees are no different. They want feedback. They want to know how they are doing at any given time. The question is, are you providing them the opportunity to have that feedback?

Believe it or not, the vast majority of your employees want to do a great job for you. The problem is that they aren't always clear on what that looks like. That absence of clarity can be extremely frustrating for someone who wants to do a great job.

There are three specific tools that you can use to ensure that your team knows the score and that you do too. Those tools are objectives, results tracking, and progress reports.

1. Objectives – What is the difference between an objective and a goal? This is a question that I get quite a bit so before we get into objectives, let's address these questions real quick. A goal is more of a long terms over-arching measure while an objective is more of a short term, specific measure.

   One way to describe the difference is with weight loss. You may have a goal to lose weight. An objective would be to say that you want to lose 15 pounds in the first 60 days. Objectives are specific and time sensitive.

   Objectives are great not only for your business as a whole but also for the individuals who work in your business.

   Giving your team objectives is a way for you to let them know what the most important aspects of their job are and what success looks like for them.

2. Tracking results – When you give your team and your business measurable results to track, it enables you to more easily assess how your team is doing. It also allows your team to know the score. One mistake that you can make with your team is assuming that they know how they are doing or how the business is doing.

   Tracking results allows you to create transformational change into your business. If you set a specific set of objectives that you feel are realistic for your business and you are behind pace, you can use this info to assess how the systems and processes are working within your business. This process can also allow you to assess how your team is doing in certain areas and identify where they can improve.

3. Employee reviews – When you have people on your team that have worked with you for a period of time, it's easy to take that relationship for granted and make assumptions about how they are doing and how we feel about them.

One mistake that you can make with your team is assuming that they know how they are doing or how the business is doing.

They need to hear how they are doing so that your relationship will remain healthy and productive.

One of the ways that I can best illustrate this is with the relationship with my wife. Regardless of how long we have been married and how good our relationship appears to be, it's still important for my wife to hear that I appreciate her. Your employees are no different. They need to hear how they are doing so that your relationship will remain healthy and productive.

When you use these three tools effectively, you now have an open line of communication with your employees that enables you to build effective relationships and your team to be more productive.

EXERCISE IN DISCOVERY

1. What is your system for tracking results in your business?

_____

_____

_____

_____

2. How could you do a better job setting objectives for your business and for your team?

_____

_____

_____

_____

3. If your team knows and understands the score and where they are at, how do you think that will affect their performance?

_____

_____

_____

_____

a business by design and not default

How do you create successful outcomes in your business? It doesn't happen by accident. You have a lot to do with the success or failure of your business. For some this news is inspiring. For other it's terrifying. Business success starts with being intentional and designing the process and outcomes for your business.

It's easy to fall into a trap of complacency or to get into a state of overwhelm and allow things to happen in your business that you don't want to happen. This happens when you decide that you don't want to confront employee behavior and you "let it slide." This happens when you don't carve out real time to work on your business. This happens when you don't look at your financials, create a budget and have a financial plan.

Here's the good news.

You can literally start changing this tomorrow. You can create a management plan and philosophy that fits the mission, vision, and values of your business. You can work on your business. You can learn the financial numbers. You can create an engaged team. If any of these areas are missing in your business, you can change it.

Success in your business starts with you and your vision. For some, this is why you started a business in the first place. For others, the thought of having this much power to affect outcomes seems like a daunting proposition.

Every single business owner who has run a business for any number of years has felt overwhelmed at times and has been complacent. Long-term successful businesses are able to overcome this, and you can, too. You can't do it alone, which is why you spent so much time reading about how to connect and engage the team that you have behind you.

Use this guide to go out and create value on a massive scale. Create value for your clients, your team, and the community around you. Use this guide to create the type of freedom that you always envisioned your business creating for you. Most of all, use this guide to help you be the leader for your business that you were born to be.

the next step

"I came to The Business Blueprint as someone who knows a lot about my field, but next to nothing about running a business and you gave me the tools and personal guidance I needed to succeed. With your information and personal guidance on my side, it didn't take long before I had the faith and knowledge to know that I could actually do this!"

–Duane

If you like the ideas we've presented in this report… and you feel your business could benefit from an improved experience, let us help you.

Register for your FREE TXD Analysis (a $397 value).

As soon as you request it, we'll send you a thorough questionnaire that will help us better understand your business.

Then, we can get on the phone and analyze where your business is at right now, and where you'd like to be.

We'll look at areas you can improve and give you actionable, key steps you can take to make a positive difference.

Some of the things you'll learn:

- How to have a team that works together and inline with your vision
- How to communicate more effectively with your team
- Create your management style and strategies to ensure that your style shows up in your business.
- Putting together a winning culture in your business
- Simple ways to use your team more effectively so you are working more in what you do best.

By the time we're done, you'll have better focus and be able to take purposeful action.

Register for your FREE TXD Analysis (a $397 value) today:

GET MY ANALYSIS

For your free analysis, click above or visit
thebizblueprint.com/business-success-analysis

reviews of TXD and the Business Blueprint

One thing that I discovered is that the little things matter. I now have tools to build better relationships with my team. Working with Brandon is essential if you want to be a better leader and a business owner.

Dr Jim Bentz
Fidalgo Island Health Center

In a recent management training session with Brandon, I learned that I need to get more feedback from my team as well as get their input on the goals of the office. I am also clear on what I want out of my business and now have a plan for how to put this together.

Dr Jennifer Moran
Moran Family Dentistry

I realized that we were not being powerful managers and that we hold the key to our team's motivation. We are clear on how to manage our team, how to engage and empower our team as well as how to make our team meetings more fun. In addition to that, I feel like we have a better process from confronting our team and handling it effectively.

Khou Graffeo
Parkview Chiropractic Center

I recently attended a management workshop put together by Brandon Allen and walked away with a better understanding of how to delegate to my team and more clarity on my next step in business.

Dr. Dean Potapinski
Confederation Chiropractic Clinic

It was helpful to think about what it looked like to scale my business for future growth and breaking down the components of a successful business. In addition to that, I learned the importance of connecting with my team and building relationships on an individual level.

Dr. Donna Williams
Morningside Dental

Notes

_____
_____
_____
_____
_____
_____
_____
_____
_____
_____
_____
_____
_____
_____
_____
_____
_____
_____
_____
_____
_____
_____
_____
_____

www.ingramcontent.com/pod-product-compliance
Lightning Source LLC
Chambersburg PA
CBHW050436180526
45159CB00006B/2558